Almost
to the
End

Almost to the End

The Shorter Poems: New and Old

Brewster Chamberlin

The New
Atlantian Library

THE NEW ATLANTIAN LIBRARY
is an imprint of
ABSOLUTELY AMAZING eBOOKS

Published by Whiz Bang LLC, 926 Truman Avenue, Key West, Florida 33040, USA.

Almost to the End copyright © 2015 Sunrise Driven, Inc. Electronic compilation/ paperback edition copyright © 2016 by Whiz Bang LLC.

All rights reserved. No part of this book may be reproduced, scanned, or transmitted in any form or by any means, electronic or mechanical, including photocopying, recording, or any information storage and retrieval system, without permission in writing from the publisher. Please do not participate in or encourage piracy of copyrighted materials in violation of the author's rights. Purchase only authorized ebook editions.

Names, characters, places, and incidents either are the product of the author's imagination or are used fictitiously, and any resemblance to actual persons, living or dead, businesses, companies, events, or locales is entirely coincidental. While the author has made every effort to provide accurate information at the time of publication, neither the publisher nor the author assumes any responsibility for errors, or for changes that occur after publication. Further, the publisher does not have any control over and does not assume any responsibility for author or third-party websites or their contents. How the ebook displays on a given reader is beyond the publisher's control.

For information contact:
Publisher@AbsolutelyAmazingEbooks.com

ISBN-13: 978-0692673478 (New Atlantian Library, The)
ISBN-10: 0692673474

For
Dean Chamberlin
brother, friend and critic

Almost to the End

Haiku doesn't answer questions, mon,
   they ask them.

        - Eden the Perfect Bartender
        at the Kyoto Edge Bar, 1922

Table of Contents

Preface i
Shorter Poems 1981 – 2015 1
Haiku-Like Poems 2013 – 2015 33

Preface

These Haiku-like poems gathered here, scattered leaves in a pile as it were, represent nighttime thoughts and inspirations written down whilst reading Sam Hamill's translations in *The Sound of Water: Haiku by Bashō, Buson, Issa, and Other Poets* (Boston: Shambala, 2000). Some of them are actually based on the work of these poets, but most are simply inspired by them. Others come from my own inspirations.

The older short poems (they are usually dated) in the first section of this book I've written over the years and do not appear in my previous collection *Situation Reports on the Emotional Equipoise* (2007); nor with one exception to they appear in the collection *Shorts of All Sorts: Selected Prose and Poems* (2013).

There is sufficient reason why some haiku resemble aphorisms, and often contain enlightening contradictions.

The poet Issa (1762-1826) wrote (in Hamill's translation):

> So many flea bites,
> but on her lovely young skin
> they are beautiful.

Key West, November 2015

Shorter Poems
1981 - 2015

Almost to the End

Portaria, Greece

One night in the summer
    we drove to the village above the harbor
where cottages hang on the mountainside –
    pools of light in the deep black sky,
cars crouch silently in the streets –
    Chariots of our time awaiting centurions –
Careful goats freely roam the lanes –
    Memories of bloody sacrifice.

Tourists at heart we step cautiously
    on paths where schoolbook figures
wore out their cranky leather sandals
    discussing the stars' comforting behavior.
There are no analogies today and
    our symbols, too, repeat theirs,
no burden is too light for them to bear;
    classic references no longer suffice.

Alone on the paths in our own present
    we have no recourse to literature;
we drink new wine – bemused, nostalgic,
    while the freighters come and go
in the darkened harbor far below
    winking at us through the night.

                        Washington DC, 1981

Brewster Chamberlin

Night Blues

At midnight in Barcelona
birds chirp but do not sing
in the early softness of summer.
dreams of the span between
Sête and Collioure's old port hotel
lull sleep until the frigo's whine
blocks the streetlamp's globular shine.
Too soon we're back on the pavement
earning a loving again.

1982

Almost to the End

Orchestra Rehearsal

The piece commenced with blue tinged chord
strummed on a Spanish guitar over which an oboe
began to whine fluttery complaints against fate
until a wail of oddly noted brass
anchored in this world
only by three baritone saxophones
snuffed the oboe out before
turning to the tympani
to make their displeasure clear.

1982

Brewster Chamberlin

She Offered Me a Broken Pillow

She offered me a broken pillow
for my aching head
    and
I lay down and rested my broken head
on her aching pillow
at the seacoast of Bohemia.
                      Tavel, 1983

Almost to the End

In Provence

From the bedroom window
It was difficult
To sense anything
But the whomp beat
Of the mistral.

                                        Tavel, 1983

Brewster Chamberlin

À Picasso

Age alone did not cut him down

He'd already lived beyond time

Knowledge stopped his brain at last

Hard enough no longer able to do the acrobatics

That dominated his old years but

Knowing the hand could no longer etch them

Cancelled the purpose and he died

The hard black eyes, deep as coal,

That knew everything yet could laugh

Except at one final piece of knowledge.

                    Avignon, July 7, 1983

Almost to the End

Amilie in Transit

And so,
stuffing her handbag
with French dead letters,
blonde Amilie move by a
circuitous route to Corsica
whence she never returned.

1985

Brewster Chamberlin

Abed with the Flu

There's only one thing worse than being in bed with
the flu and that's being in bed with the flu when guests
are present in the house.
    Ancient Scottish proverb
    Read
    Whilst abed
    With empty head
    And the flu

        Scumbler
        A Marriage of True Minds
        Djuna
    And, as always,
        Ellmann's Joyce.

October 21, 1985

Almost to the End

Autumn Leaves

In the autumn
Wet leaves stick
To their predestined image
And lie defeated
Strewn about the street

Capitol Hill
November 1987

Brewster Chamberlin

Baths and Showers

Baths are not
Meant to cleanse
But arouse or relax us
Showers are for cleansing
One's body
At least in any rational
Culture.

                      Capitol Hill, 1987

Almost to the End

If Bookshelves Groan

If bookshelves groan
It must be with pleasure –
Imagine being weighed down
By beauty and truth in print –
Let us pray
Buckled by Joyce and Prévert
Testing the strength of your muscles –
What delicious agony
Strain my tendons, Petrarch
With all your mental Laura lust.
After all
It is what one carries that counts.

Paris, November 14, 1987

Brewster Chamberlin

In My Quarter of the City

In my quarter of the city
When it rains it sometimes
Sparkles on the pavement
Sometimes the raucous voices
On the street do not disturb
Sometimes there's a parking space
On the street where we live
In my quarter of the city.
Barring a catastrophe
The market's always open on Saturdays.
              Cibola! Cibola! Cibola!
Memories are short here
A decade is a century
Row after row houses brightly
Colored in sub-urban finery
Dans mon beau quartier
              Indeed.

           Capitol Hill, November 1987

Almost to the End

Morning's Dream

Unfurl, my spirit, like a flag at dawn
Treat me to a charming bite
On prick's end in the crack of the lawn
Where the entrance is never too tight.

Brewster Chamberlin

Song of the Naiads

Just me, just you
Everybody's in the pickle jar
What else is new?

Almost to the End

Our House

There are no vistas here –
The side neighbors are but feet away
The house sits too near the street
With no demarcation sidewalks

Sitting on the back porch
Several feet from the wood fence
We see splotches of the clear blue sky
Through the palm trees and hibiscus

The vistas to the ocean and the gulf
We envision in our mind's eye
Where they are almost as inviting
If we keep reality at a decent distance.

                              December 1, 2006

Brewster Chamberlin

Sun Maddened

Here in the Caribbean sun
After the hurricanes have gone
The shadows are yellow and green
In the visions of a maddened mind
On William Street in the shade.

                        11.X.2009

Almost to the End

We are Free Men

We are free men
We build cathedrals
We write classic songs
We paint expensive oils
We carve eternal sculptures
We mow the lawn.

May 2010

Brewster Chamberlin

The Rhyming Dervish Song

Won't you be my Lorna Doone
Or I'll end up crazy as a loon
Without a lilting song of tune
Up there in that skyward balloon
To be so all alone on the old chilled moon
With only a lone guardian goon
Dressed in red, green and maroon.
O let me be that dancing fool
Before I end up a farflung ghoul
Tripping my way like a demented mule
In frantic moves without a decent rule
O let me be that prancing fool
      Or else you know why!

                    November 10, 2010

Almost to the End

The Last Saloon

Easily missed with open eyes
If you walk too fast past all the lies
If you're searching for the truth
                            Forget it
Keep on ambling down the sunbright street
To the darkening end stop
                            Packaged so neat
For there's your eternal goal
Where you can hide like a mole
And wash your joys with uncut whiskey
To face the final end of the mystery
For this is, after all,
                            The Edge Bar
The last saloon by far.

                    16. II. 13

Brewster Chamberlin

Where We Live

We live behind the orange door
(handpainted twice without permission
from local authorities)
in the submarine space
of a conch house
(that means small, mon, small)
on the end-of-the-road island
laced with mangos and Poinciana's
where we are happy and spacy
and a cat named Nicole lives with us.

                              26. II. 13

Almost to the End

Books

I like books in every room
for me they are a thrill and boon
stacked in corners
piled on tables
arranged along the shelves
books in the house
make me feel needed
to read them
to dust them
to smell them.
How would they survive
                      Without me?

Brewster Chamberlin

Kitchen Dreams

I want some burgers and fries
To match the stars in your eyes.

Never a dropped cauliflower fleurette
Never an under or overcooked scallop
To remind me of a bug I once et
Or a Cajun sauce that packs a wallop.

Mid-Century American Youth

Two middle-class white teenagers
In the back of his parents' car
He wonders how
She wonders if.

Almost to the End

Do Cats Dream?

Do cats dream
        of mice
        in the fields of plenty
Of small birds
        in the sapodilla leaves
Of dry food treats
        at the end of the day
Of hunting at night
        when their humans sleep
Of neighborhood dogs
        with uncertain intents
Or do cats dream
        of other cats at play in the grass
With satisfactory endings?

                      3. III. 2013

Brewster Chamberlin

Here on this Southern Island

Here on this southern island
watching the orange setting sun
my thoughts tumble golden
over one another
and I see so briefly
all the women
in my life
when they were young.
Bereft of reason
my mind does not distinguish
among them in hierarchy
they were all beautiful
and young
at every age.

                                        December 2014

Almost to the End

We All Slept Carefree on the Bed

We all slept carefree on the bed
until the scorpion bit her
she screamed in excruciating pain
and like a berserker
ran from the room
through her door to the porch.
When she returned home
she was not the same
a small stroke we thought
though we never found out
and sadly watched the poor kitty
at eight years old
become old and afraid
but we never stopped loving her.

March 10, 2015

Brewster Chamberlin

Does She Dream

Does she dream
Here on this tropic isle
Of the North Country
When she was young
But never easy,
Traveling those long country roads
Up toward the freezing borderland
Long time gone now.
But memories remain somewhere
Back of the mind,
Innocent when they don't intrude:
Floating down the Apple River
In those summer inner tubes
Skin as bare as fashion allowed
Flashing laughter in the sun,
And winter's tears across the land
When love is frozen in the North Country
Despite bundled up in blue parkas.

Here love basks in the sun
The summer never ends
And we are no longer young
But we are together.

April 2015

Almost to the End

At the Graveyard

The most famous line in the place
"I told you I was sick"
In a weathered plaque on the small mausoleum
The wail of an unattended fatal illness
Now fodder for the passing tourists
Whose elbows nudge one another as they grin
Appreciating the humor and move on
To the next site in the southernmost bone orchard.

April 5, 2015

Brewster Chamberlin

The Scavengers of Love

The scavengers of love
See no beauty in truth
No matter how brightly it shines
They see only a blur
They cannot understand.

Almost to the End

Old Man's Thoughts

I am old now
                            but
once I was young if not beautiful
once I had packets of energy
Now I have aches and pains
once I read deep into the night
now I fall asleep after a few pages
once I was the envy of the neighborhood
hop, skip, jump, leap into the nearest abyss
I don't regret a minute of it
but at high noon
in the still of the night
                            I do miss it.

                        May 2, 2015

Brewster Chamberlin

The Animal Kingdom

The hovering hawk
A brown and black mass
Flattened its spread wings
And plummeted at speed
After the scrambling rabbit's
Erratic trail of fear.
No contest.
      August 4, 2015

Haiku-like Poems 2013-2015

Almost the End

Looking through
old telephone numbers
so many crossed out.

The silence of the wind
on the lonely plain
dry desperation.

A single crow
upon a bare branch
omen of the end.

Brewster Chamberlin

The snow falls early
this fine year
sign of a long winter.

The cicadas cry
without thought
do they know
they're about to die?

The promise of snow
threatens my journey
to the capital of desire.

Almost the End

></p>

The humming mosquito
hunts the source
of the plum blossoms.

Snow flowers bloom
in the mirror
of winter days and nights.

The shadow of my life
follows me demanding
an answer to why.

Brewster Chamberlin

We hear bird song
in night's forest
before dawn appears.

Poverty enhances
the goal of freedom
for the wanderer.

Winter rains
even our furry cat
needs rain gear.

Almost the End

    Rain clouds bare
    the distant hills
  tell us where we are.

  Winter in the temple
    fist breaking ice
  in the early morning.

  Cherry blossoms drift
around the tidal basin
  a gift to the nation.

Brewster Chamberlin

Glowing autumn brook
wakes me at sunrise
with dream fragments.

So cold that night
ice cracking the jar
awakened me.

Skylarks do not sing
in summer days
they are too long.

Almost the End

I wonder as I wander
what is my real name
too many winter rains.

Yellow summer grasses
the big shots'
imperialist dreams.

Cherry blossoms
fall upon the dream
of empire rule.

Brewster Chamberlin

Peasants' voices
harvest songs lovelier
than city poets' works.

The hobo's remnants
would protect me
against the winter.

The wet stone sizzles
in the midday heat
a tired heart no longer beats.

Almost the End

The silly woodpecker
taps rhythmically
on the metal lamppost.

The cricket chirps
indifferent to the bodies
on the ground.

Wet between her thighs
she opens to accept
life's second demand.

Brewster Chamberlin

I think about New York
but do I want to return
without a dime.

With passing time
no earth moves in rhythm
only kind autumn slips by.

How satisfying
the summer dress
drenched with semen.

Almost the End

White drops dry
on her brown thighs
exhaustion then follows.

A single leaf falls
harbinger of autumn
winter is cold and dry.

Bitter rice icon image
black stockings and
thick thighs in water.

Brewster Chamberlin

Marie the dawn breaks
your image fades
as we awaken.

In the early morning
my chamber pot
demands fulfillment.

Clarity of mind
leads to knowledge
some of the time.

Almost the End

> Primitive animals
> brag to each other
> primitively at best.

> Winds blow all
> away as soon
> as all appears.

> The icebound river
> reluctantly gives up
> its secret dead.

Brewster Chamberlin

I cheated today
I drove the car
instead of the bike.

The cats in Athens
in danger daily
in the famine.

I reach a shoulder
to scratch an itch
and it's long gone.

Almost the End

How pedestrian
to find no satori
in the lightning flash.

Breakfast on the rooftop
in old Havana
prepares the day.

Walking so high
the mountain gorge
likes our soft shoes.

Brewster Chamberlin

Dewdrops fall
from high roofs
while the world dies.

Culture is questionable
when songs ignore
the rice harvest.

A bright new year
a bright new poem
great thought.

Almost the End

Bamboo stalks
reflect sounds
of water dropping.

A lazy moon
shines on a woman
nude in the courtyard.

The whore's cart
leaves traces on the road
the way to paradise.

Brewster Chamberlin

A cold long night
drives the poor priest
to creative endeavors.

The small fish
leaps too high
to reach the mosquitos.

I am here alone
a man visits me
we talk in the evening.

Almost the End

Silver moon passes by
the village hovels
then moves on.

Farewell everyone
I am moving down
the road to autumn.

Sudden spring wind
unexpected swift
lifts my robe.

Brewster Chamberlin

Sweet spring light rain
unable to meet the sadness
of my lonely days – too bad.

Alone at the game
my nose runs
in the chilled night.

Swallows land everywhere
on church spire or village roof
no matter they are there.

Almost the End

Evening rain squalls
shake the branches
upon which sparrows cling.

Errol Garner groans
as he pounces heavy
on the keys to his soul.

Undistinguishable fly
burns bright at the shrine
before collapsing into itself.

Brewster Chamberlin

We don't know them
but we dream of them
days so far away then.

After miles of tramping
rain crushes down the clover
as if I'd walked there.

The late autumn leaves
hide the evening crow
his cry echoes loudly.

Almost the End

Alone the monk resists
the bitter wind
and bends down to pray.

The poor farmer
has no choice
but to plant his stool
where he works.

Soft mice feet
walking on porcelain
music of cold winters.

Brewster Chamberlin

The autumn twilight
explains the pleasure
of being alone.

The woodpecker's rap
on the metal pole
frustration of the breed.

When the old conch
is blown at noon
the contest begins.

Almost the End

The old guy waits
but he's too late
the ferry left in the rain.

Our wooden icons
in the cold winter forest
would warm the homes.

Sometimes when awake
I feel like the pale moon
cold, along, and old.

Brewster Chamberlin

The moon above the funeral
   pale, round and pitted
  tells me nothing now.

In deep old age
  the greatest pleasure
singing Buddha's name.

Swarms of butterflies
  in autumn colors
leaves back on the branch.

Almost the End

What if there is a hell
pestilence and brimstone
will I go there tomorrow.

The old cat hears
The single crunch
Of the bole weevil.

Old crone lies dying
her mind in her youth
surrounded by eager boys.

Brewster Chamberlin

The house shudders and shakes
beneath Nature's angry blast
hurricane season again.

Moonlight slows
the letter's words
she weeps at the news.

Not bougainvillea
but gardenias' heavy weight
surrounds this tropic house.

Almost the End

On the island
of fresh sea breezes
her slips dry soon.

Her head pillowed
on my curved arm
under the hazy moon.

The loud bell
rudely awakens
clinging new butterfly.

Brewster Chamberlin

The new horse turds
do not disturb
red plum tree blossoms.

Heavy spring rain
sounds a skittering
of deep cello music.

Viking hat, fur coat
the image of Moondog
on New York streets.

Almost the End

On the asphalt's edge
Fallen gardenia petals
Disappear in the traffic.

At night the cute kitty
crunches bird's bones
for our morning pleasure.

The autumn wind
pimples her nude body
in the old tea house.

Brewster Chamberlin

In yellow autumn
golden breeze lifts
her kimono above the delta.

The unmuffled motor
Down our narrow lane
Frightens our small cat.

The poor poet wandering
without a chamber pot
yellow holes in white snow.

Almost the End

The sound of water
cleans my ears
the raging torrent.

Sea birds fly black
against a pale blue sky
before sunrise orange.

The beloved cat
always in the house
tiny scabs on my toes.

Brewster Chamberlin

River passes my door
carries many things
all old used flotsam.

The slightest feather
in the squaw's hair
knows the difference
between wind and breeze.

The old blind man
stares at the sea
expecting his wife to return.

Almost the End

In the lonely corn field
they sleep together
the whore and the monk.

The sound of water
moves the frog
into the depth of the lake.

She follows the trail
endlessly to nowhere
abandoned by all
except the moon.

Brewster Chamberlin

The cicadas cry beautifully
only when they know
they are dying.

My tired horse
refused to move
beyond the lunch stand.

The wild sea
over Puget Sound
heaven's river flows.

Almost the End

    The firefly glows
       in the dark
   but fades in the sun
  and pleases no one.

   Cormorant drunk
   on freedom to fly
    into the future.

   Exhausted I found
   a room in her inn
   spread thighs of a
    fool's paradise.

Brewster Chamberlin

Among those there
for the sunset
not one beautiful face.

The lonely dove moans
through the long night
the moon shines indifferent.

The thunder bowls
around the sky
a river of sound.

Almost the End

    The lonely monk
   fell out of paradise
up into the whore's arms.

   Autumn evening
   early this year
  empty wet lanes.

 The ficus in the rain
leans down to the lane
drops colors on the porch.

Brewster Chamberlin

Rain borne wind
soaks my hair
and closes my eyes.

The sunrise doesn't smell
but the rainbow
sheds many colors.

Late winter desires
bring images of spring
bird songs on the wing.

Almost the End

Watching the TV
with one eye
she fingers her clit
and is happy.

The mountain tree
bends so far down
the swallow moves on.

Rain-laden clouds
in darkening autumn
old age begins.

Brewster Chamberlin

Rain season ends
autumn colors flourish
joy spreads in flashes.

Great lilac blooms
shelter the old man
behind the fence.

From all around
the Tidal Basin
once a year
cherry blossoms fall.

Almost the End

All the road's hobos
endless life stories
cactus blooms in the night.

Buddha has a birthday
or so we are told
but what do we know?

Along the wood pews
rough bruised hands
clasped in prayer.

Brewster Chamberlin

Those who pray
in the church pews
do not see Christ's tears.

The urban ruin
can only be described
by one of its residents.

Full autumn moon
brings high tides
awash in dead sea grass.

Almost the End

>   Plucking gray hairs
>   from her lovely head
>   my love continues.

>   I move through time
>   without a thought
>   of cleaning the house.

>   We smelled the jasmine
>   on the spring nights
>   longing for summer.

Brewster Chamberlin

As autumn nears
we long and think
of our tousled beds.

The old scarecrow
in the derelict field
memories of the harvest.

The great sapodilla
in the public courtyard
indifferent to humans' gaze.

Almost the End

       The yellow moon
       turns vaguely white
       blinding those looking.

       Wild duck's cry
       over evening's waters
       is soon gone away.

       Thick wafts of night jasmine
       disturb my ears
       where are the church bells?

Brewster Chamberlin

Hands in the fields
soon grow tired
they belong to humans.

No winter here
we all sweat
happy year round.

Sky bound sea bird
sings its loneliness
with earth bound songs.

Almost the End

New Year's day
cold loneliness
but warm thoughts.

After I'm gone
my songs alone
are left to wander
amongst the hills.

In the evening
bright white gardenias
fade to autumn yellow.

Brewster Chamberlin

Rain falls heavily
on your own river
you imagine the flood.

Obese men
do not destroy
plum blossoms in bloom.

Yellow corn
in green stalks
food for winter.

Almost the End

Bright green leaf
after night's rain
dry brown tomorrow.

Poverty sounds
with handsaw rasp
in the digital age.

Bat darts back and forth
urgent need
for moonlit plum.

Brewster Chamberlin

No ideogram alone
signifies my yearning
for eternal love.

Rain falls softly on grass
and parched earth
absorbs all the drops.

The bath mist rises
silvery in the moonlight
she encompasses his erection.

Almost the End

The workers in the field
so pathetic in poverty
I am so bored.

The beggar on the road
an empty battered tin
pray for me.

In my torn cloak
fleas spend a night
no longer alone.

Brewster Chamberlin

Swift silver moon
so fast in the morning
gone in the evening.

The beige gecko
I tried to chase
the cat achieved.

The small piece of color
yellow in the autumn grass
suddenly moves.

Almost the End

    Watch the deep sea
    for buried memories
O father where have you gone?

The fools cut down
the Australian pines
ignorance rules.

The moonlight way
luminous, hazy
leads us nowhere.

Brewster Chamberlin

The osprey's shrill
plaintive call
for mate or child.

The monks knew
a lot of reading
little comprehension.

The days fluttering away
butterflies quickly passing
then gone with no memories
of ever having been here.

Almost the End

      In my village
      my old house
a rose thorn of pain.

    In the blue rain
    cherry blossoms
hide the one who remains.

Nightingale's swoon song
    the mango drops
    he wakes alone.

Brewster Chamberlin

Young man leaving the village
cannot see beyond it
does not hear
the lark singing.

Morning dew on the bough
the snail slips and slides
the sun soon rises.

In this village
a chapel with no priest
but O the steak-frites.

Almost the End

The hoagy skylark
croons its love song
across the low plains.

The skylark knows no limit
to the village edge
sings songs without limit.

When the sweet young girl
reached her first orgasm
the skylarks sang.

Brewster Chamberlin

She gave him the Judah's kiss
 but he didn't realize
  the nature of it
 until it was too late.

 After the storm
 sunlight silence
 a seagull laugh.

Moonshine enlightens
 the dull gray day
and the sky turns yellow.

Almost the End

      The courting frog
      cannot long fool
      the seagull's song.

Just when the sermon
has bored us to tears
the cuckoo raspberries.

Fearing the storm
all the living people
scurry out of town.

Brewster Chamberlin

After admonishing us
to hold our breath
our host died.

Spring cherry trees
lose their pink blossoms
to our helpless dismay.

The cool summer rain
bends the towering pines
but does not break them.

Almost the End

Cherry blossoms remain
unmoved by the church bell
calling the parishioners.

The poor man's house
open to nature's moods
freezes in winter.

The derelict chapel
at the village edge
fills with squirling leaves
on winter evenings.

Brewster Chamberlin

The obscure young poet
knows no difference
his nose and a plum.

Marie the dawn breaks
I see you there
and I must weep with joy.

Seeing the clear blue sky
the jumping salmon
misses the rocks below.

Almost the End

The apples of Cézanne
all alone on the table
need no atmosphere.

Into the midday silence
the iguana intrudes
the sound of its lunch.

The grey tree rat
leaps from the branch
to the roof
ignorant of electricity.

Brewster Chamberlin

The traveler's palm
spreads its wide leaves
hiding the insects
eating its heart.

Along the long winding road
the traveler's tiring way
full moon brightens.

The lovely proud cat
brings in the dead bird
does its mate mourn?

Almost the End

On the artist's bed
the smell of turpentine
and erotic remnants
of the last night.

Cold distant moon
streams of chilled breaths
autumn leaves burned
another year ends.

The orchid's end
in summer heat
teaches how to die.

Brewster Chamberlin

Green gecko's eye
reflects wide blue sky
and drifting white clouds.

What is the banker's
vast wealth to me?
Immorality in high places.

The hurricane's terrible winds
whip the strongest palm trees
and drive the sea deep inland.

Almost the End

In the southern tropics
no winter here
so how to greet the spring?

If she hadn't left
she'd listen to my
inconsiderate complaints
and feel the sunrise warmth.

Open winter window
rain on my sheets
gift of Nature's bounty.

Brewster Chamberlin

Winter here for me
early evening darkness
and open windows.

The woman on the beach
exercises naked
in the gold sunset
enriching my life.

The young kitten
already knows well
nature's various ways.

Almost the End

Don't step on that gecko
the little guy
is completely innocent.

Erroll Garner's
flat pressed hair
does nothing to the music.

Happiness has no relation
to a nose with a bird
blue or not.

Brewster Chamberlin

In the moonlight
she stands waiting
against the garden wall.

Blow man blow,
the old man yelled
bliss in the smoky club.

Young brown wrens
return to the nest
seeking safety and salvation.

Almost the End

My concentration
broken by her image
planting swamp rice.

Along the rim of empire
we stagger forward
careless of our steps.

Dogs barking at night
frogs croaking at twilight
saying they are alive.

Brewster Chamberlin

The lonely old monk
desired the girl
but accepted the woman.

Winter winds
blow hard on my face
in what hell will I end?

How I envy
the mosquito that
sucked blood from her thigh.

Almost the End

    After we've gone
the cats prowl the yard
   hungry as always.

     Some languages
have no word for home
   how sad is that?

Arrival of the new year
moon rising at night
simplicity of nature.

Brewster Chamberlin

Cracks along the rim of empire
dangerous for walkers
tread lightly or fall.

Drunk with god
the perfect Buddha
lies at the roadside
alone with her thoughts.

What happens to the bees
all gold yellow buzzing
after the beekeeper dies?

Almost the End

Planet of tribulations
fishing in the back country
a world of calm and quiet.

When I have no teeth left
I'll drink too much
rain will fall through the roof.

Gardenia tree blossoms
chill winter winds
calm down to stasis.

Brewster Chamberlin

On this island
at the end of the pier
sunrise surprises us.

The cat moves slowly
through the day
at night a fierce huntress.

The kitchen means
warmth and bread
drawing us into the smells.

Almost the End

The heavy iguana
ungainly and ugly
how does it climb trees?

Human ambition
knows no limit
man lands on the moon.

A deep pleasure
of a man's old age
watching the girls
dressed in their summer clothes.

Brewster Chamberlin

The flowers of evil
will not teach
anyone how to die.

On tropical islands
seasons do change
only for the subtle eye.

Pure snow flakes
are a luxury
the tropics cannot afford.

Almost the End

When my lovely cat
kills the small blue bird
does its mate mourn?

Does the desert cactus
yearn for water
beneath the endless sun?

I begin the day
with bicycle rides
and glorious sunrises.

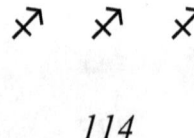

Thank you for reading.

Please review this book. Reviews help others find Absolutely Amazing eBooks and inspire us to keep providing these marvelous tales.

If you would like to be put on our email list to receive updates on new releases, contests, and promotions, please go to AbsolutelyAmazingEbooks.com and sign up.

About the Author

After completing a well-received doctoral dissertation on modern German history, Chamberlin spent several decades of his life working as a historian, archivist, university teacher, lecturer, poet, essayist and writer of longer and shorter fictions while living in Manhattan, Germany, France (Provence), Italy, Washington DC and Greece. In 2001, after 17 years, he retired from an executive position at the U.S. Holocaust Memorial Museum in Washington DC to move with his wife Lynn-Marie Smith to Key West, Florida to concentrate on writing. His most recent books are *Paris Now and Then: Memoirs, Opinions and a Companion to the City of Light for the Literate Traveler* (2002, revised edition 2004); *Mediterranean Sketches: Fictions, Memories and Metafictions* (2005); (with Nance Frank) *Mario Sanchez: Once Upon a Way of Life* (2006); *A Chronology of the Life and Times of Lawrence Durrell* (2007); *Situation Reports on the Emotional Equipoise: Collected Poems 1959-2006* (2007); *Radovic's Dilemma. A Mediterranean Thriller* (2009); and *The Time in Tavel: An Informal Illustrated Memoir of a Sojourn in Provence* (2010). *Shorts of All Sorts. Selected Prose and Poems* (2013), *Travels in Greece and France and the Durrell School of Corfu Seminars. Travelogues and Lectures* (2013), *A Paris Chapbook* (2013) and *The Hemingway Log. A Chronology of His Life and Times* (2015).

Chamberlin has worked at the Key West Art and Historical Society as a volunteer historian and research associate since 2002 and also served on the Durrell School of Corfu board of directors and faculty, and has been and is a board member of several Key West non-profit organizations.

The New Atlantian Library

NewAtlantianLibrary.com
or AbsolutelyAmazingEbooks.com
or AA-eBooks.com

www.ingramcontent.com/pod-product-compliance
Lightning Source LLC
Chambersburg PA
CBHW050834160426
43192CB00010B/2028